hell broke loose

hell broke loose

poems on the holocaust

by warren gaston

hell broke loose

poems on the holocaust

ISBN 13: 978-1791732097

Printed in the United States of America

CONTENTS

PREFACE

I did not set out to write these poems. The first poem came to me. Hard poems often come uninvited, stepping out of the shadows of the unconscious. The line "I would like to believe the Holocaust never happened" arrived one summer morning on a mountain top. I quickly scrawled the poem in my notebook.

Even though the poem was unsolicited, my mind was not unprepared. I grew up in a Protestant household in the 1940's and 1950's. My father and uncle, both WWII veterans, were haunted by the Holocaust. How could this singular crime against humanity take place in a civilized and Christian country? How could this well organized and systematic massacre of millions of people become a nation's policy?

These questions were asked often enough to impress upon my young mind that some horror had been committed, not in the distant past, but recently, by people not unlike me. As I grew older I wondered what my life would have been like if I lived in Nazi Germany? Would I have been swept up in the tsunami of groupthink? Would I have been seduced by the promise of a thousand year utopia? Would I have the courage to stand against this delusion carried out by industrialized mass murder?

These poems are my poor attempt to explore the noxious ethical atmosphere of Nazi Germany, breathed-in by its citizens, thus distorting the individual's moral vision, seeing personal and tribal advantage at any cost as the highest good, and receiving permission to take that advantage at the peril of others.

Today I am alarmed by the power of malevolent rhetoric which has awakened so much slumbering hatred around the world and in the United States of America.

The philosopher Theodore Adorno wrote: "To write poetry after Auschwitz is barbaric." Many think Adorno was right and I am one of them. But I also think he was wrong. Adorno was right in his concern that fine language and articulate insight might soften and make reasonable the monstrous extermination machine called the Holocaust. What words are adequate to engage the gravity of this unparalleled atrocity? And what is the purpose of these words? Warning? Pity? Righteousness indignation? And what about the possibility that understanding the crime in some way excuses it?

But all of human experience, including horrific and orderly evil, needs to be investigated to its dark core. Words that confront us with surgical precision and emotional impact are necessary to wake us so that the not so distant past does not become the not so distant future. Poetry is the raw language of penetrating insight and emotional resonance.

The poems in the first person singular or plural are my attempt to understand myself inside the propaganda and terror machine of Nazi Germany. Some observe the quasi-mystical element of Nazi propaganda. Two deal with the fascination/revulsion of the Jewish poet Paul Celan for the German philosopher Martin Heidegger, who remained silent about his Nazi affiliation even after the war.

The Russian composer, Dmitri Shostakovich, wrote of the famous Yevtushenko poem *Babi Yar**:

> "People knew about Babi Yar before
> Yevtushenko's poem, but they were silent.
> Art destroys silence."

May these poems help destroy this deadly silence. We must not allow hell to break loose again.

Babi Yar – a ravine near the city of Kiev where in September of 1941 the German Einsatzgruppen and Ukrainian collaborators murdered thousands of Jews.

Warren Gaston is a poet and teacher. He retired after forty years serving congregations as a Protestant minister. His writing can be found on his website, poetrybreaksthings.com.

Denying the Holocaust

I would like to believe the Holocaust never happened
and except for the overwhelming weight of evidence,
I could.

I would like to believe the Holocaust never happened,
that *Stille Nacht* was not sung beneath the chimneys of
Auschwitz,
that the beech trees of Buchenwald did not puke poison in
spring,
that the burghers of Munich did not plug their ears to the
weeping of Dachau,
that wolves prowling the fences of Treblinka
could still howl through milk teeth without shame.

I would like to believe the Holocaust never happened,
and if I overlook arms inked with numbers,
shoes untied from countless feet, clothes missing bodies,
glasses missing eyes, gold missing teeth, veins missing blood,
I could.

I would like to believe the Holocaust never happened,
and if I believe the strange ovens merely baked a strange
bread,
if I disregard the bone smoke pouring into
    Beethoven's sky,
        Goethe's sky,
            Schiller's sky,
if I ignore snow thick with human ash,
I could.

I would like to believe the Holocaust never happened,
and if I knew boys with church faces could not stretch
barbed-wire,
if I was certain murderers could not smile,
could not smooth the mussed hair of daughters while holding
matches,
could not settle sweetly onto their nakedly witless wives,
I could.

I would like to believe the Holocaust never happened,
that inside Nazi Germany,
the frenzied scream of Hitler did not vaporize brains,
the efficiency of Himmler did not mesmerize clerks,
the swaying bray of Goebbels did not tranquilize clerics,
that the stench of death was not endured for the promise of
roses,
and if blue-eyed blonds had not swallowed de-moralizing
medicine,
I could believe the Holocaust never happened.

I would like to believe the Holocaust never happened,
that photographs were underexposed causing darkness,
that historians wore suits made of facts turned inside out,
so their lie could be easily reversed, corrected, set straight,
proving once and for all the Holocaust never happened.

But to believe the Holocaust never happened,
we would need to commit more crimes against truth,
massacre details; dates, times, locations, railroad schedules,
iron rails and wooden ties, order forms, ink, telephone wire,
canisters, protocols, rules and regulations.

We would need to dispossess the heinous facts
to make room for a falsified fiction.
We would need to eviscerate history
until innocence could no longer be born.

The Art of Not Knowing

How could we know
with nothing around us
but evidence?

Try as we might,
we did not discover
what we didn't want to know.

Kristallnacht November 9-10, 1938

Air,
transparent, now brittle,
splintered glass.

Night's fluid dark
hardened to stone.

The virus of hate was deliberately released.
A plague of permission broke out,
a moral cholera,
weakening a resistant '*no*',
favoring an infectious '*yes*.'

As the disease progressed
allowance crippled restraint,
uncivil advantages were taken.
What was against the law became the law.

In the streets men spoke a language of snarls,
glass broke,
hot venom spilled igniting books,
a centuries old craze now loose
sent scorched pages

        flying,

fire-blackened crows,
into the sky.

Doubtless thugs,
infected with a virulent strain
of advantageous belief,
invited ill-starred men
abruptly to leave their homes
wearing nightshirts of incredulous shock.

Fury cooled until rage became reasonable,
plans were made,
factories built for industrialized death,
corpses manufactured by the thousands,
commodities traded on the white market.

Husbands and fathers,
children, mothers, wives,

                    disappeared

into the malicious smoke
of hollow caustic
cataclysmic years.

Hitler Before the Mirror

Hitler -
      histrionic before the mirror

         gesticulation

             face clench
             lip twist
             eye stab
             head cock
             fist thrust
             heart throb

        practice,
        practice
        practice

                the voice
                the voice
                the voice

     shot from a strangled mouth

       of a ventriloquist

     belching the swallowed dead

cadence of cadavers

       shrill sopranic thunder

            skill
        kill

   hypodermic   epidemic

        skin under
     skin under
skin under
        sunder

the madness from the man

                blunder
                                slumber
                poise

                                pois-
                        on

          adoration

                                adore nation

                duplicate
                triplicate
                quadruplicate

     copied carbon

          breath after sycophantic breath

a million voices

          echo off his mirror

                rage

racing sclerotic veins

                        on
                on
          on

hysterical angel

          germ
man

          hit
lure.

Chameleon

*"The sad truth is that most evil is done by people who never
make up their minds to be good or evil."*
— Hannah Arendt

Is who we are where we are?
Does our where become our who?
Is where we are who we are?

Our *Dasein*.

Our moral destination.
Our immoral location.

The chameleon's adaptive absorption
into the color of its space.

We are not bad people.
We wear the face of our place.

We are a dreamy people,
traumatized by Hitler's *Traum*,
a white blazing future of German stars,
the Reich a black hole.

Auschwitz. Dachau. Treblinka. Sobibor.

Event horizons. Points of no return.
We hold an idealized idea of ourselves.

Choosing neither good nor bad,
we drifted choiceless as a cloud
in the wind of the Nazi crowd.
We did not overcome inertia with an act.

The Architect of Hell

If I was a famous architect,
hired by God to revamp hell,
I would first search for precedents.

I would quickly reject
the Hades of the Greeks
with Charon ferrying across the Styx
and the Sheol of the Jews
full of revered ancestors
as being too mythologically rich
to serve as eternal punishment,
let alone damnation.

I would consider the Valley of Hinnon
outside Jerusalem, Gehenna,
the place of fire and stench and human sacrifice
in the adoration of Moloch.

But even a proposal based on that hideous fester
would be crumpled and tossed as woefully inadequate.

Not until I turned to Auschwitz and Treblinka
would I have a worthy antecedent for my redesign.

I would insist on a construction gang
of entirely broken people, confused,
then fused into a single monomanic will.

With blueprints and perpetrators in place,
I would begin the execution of God's new hell.

1. This hell would be efficient and logical.
2. This hell would substitute numbers for names.
3. This hell would house the innocent.
4. This hell would amuse the guardians at the gate.
5. In this hell devils would enjoy the pleasures of atrocity.
6. This hell would be dictated by principles, procedures,
    protocols.
7. This hell would be managed by uniforms.
8. This hell would make God repent of forgiveness.
9. This hell would make God weep for heaven.
10. This hell has been accomplished.

Warm Italy 1939

A ghost of dead Romans.
A defiant tree flowers.
The tree is cut down.
Sidewalks and dust.

A bell rings then stops ringing.

A drum resists being beaten
but is beaten anyway.
The sticks rape the skin of the drum.

Somewhere in my heart
an old Jew begins to grasp what is happening.

The order becomes even more orderly,
neat, reasonable, vicious.

Machines and men.
Who can tell?
Rods bound together.

An ill wind blows

Rome

clean of irony.

An ambiguous baker
bakes an ambiguous bread.

     The bread confuses.
          The baker is shot.

Garlic is peeled.
Wine poured.
Wedding cake swivels on a hook.
Biting brides are dragged away
from private convictions.

Ants are happy
in this involuntary world.

Eva Braun

Berghof, Bavaria

Stretching mountain vastness,
no real or rumored world beyond the peaks.

Eva Braun had no clue the fledgling
sparrow of conscience was trapped
in the immense room of her miniature life.
No wing flapping panic hard
against the invisibilities of glass.

Eva practiced ignorance
like saints practice prayer,
wanting no more than to know less
than was necessary,
and then some.

She held malice toward none,
and love for little
but the brittle fantasy of Hitler's hope.

Fuhrersbunker, Berlin

On April 29, 1945
she spoke her vows and married death
in a cave beneath Berlin
where night did not differ from day.
Der Fuhrer kissed his lady toy
and fed her cake which left a frosted
mustache beneath her nose.

Her brief subterranean honeymoon
was spent down
two flights
of dim lit steps
beneath the ground.

That night Eva dropped her Bavarian smock
to lay under the chemicals of *der Fuhrer's* body,

hydrochloric blood,
sulfurous breath,
neon nerves chasing shadows from his skull,
tin skin worn over the rattle of stacked bones,
mind bleached clean of the moral stain of doubt.

Was she in love with the Aryan myth
or the Jew-hating man
when she felt his ice cold cock
half search for warmth?

Her ardor did not cool.
She performed her wifely favor
thirty hours before she married death again.

The Wannsee Conference: January 20, 1942

Tuesday.
          Cold.
                    Berlin,
    near,
         the war
far away.

The villa staffed and ready.

Important.
         Essential.
         Consequential.

Sun light glistened
on the ripples of Lake Wannsee,
snow cold white on the roof.

Fifteen chairs around a conference table.
The table - - - - - - - - - - polished.
The glassware - - - - - - - polished.
The cutlery - - - - - - - - - polished.
The uniform buttons - - - polished.
Shoes and boots - - - - - - polished.

After lunch dishes were removed
on polished silver trays.

There was work to be done,
plans made, protocol established,
policy polished to a sheen.

                Die Judenfrage.

What should be done with the Jews?

Each man received statistics
on 8½ x 11, white, 24 pound paper.
How many Jews and where?

The goal – Estonia,
                    a country *Judenfrei*.

Eighty five minutes later –

                    die Endlosung.

The adjournment.

                    Auf Wiedersehen.

Fifteen chairs pushed back
by thirty *Sieg Heil* feet.

Wannsee Conference (2)

When the question *why*
is answered with a lie . . .

When the question *why* has been
asked & answered good enough for a thousand years . . .

when the question *why* is
shown to the door of the conference room . . .

When the question *why* is
starved for affection . . .

When the question *why* falls
in the street searching for a friend . . .

When the question *why* dies
lonely of grief . . .

When the question *why*
vanishes as smoke into air . . .

The questions of grave concern
are *what* and *how*.

Night Train to Nowhere

Fright trains

       forced

into unspeakable duties.

At the throttle,
             a mask
             on a husk

       staring into fog.

       Night
            whistle
                     wail,
   sound
          stretched

disappearing north into silence.

         Smoke belch,
coal ash,

       cinders in eyes.

Cattle cars.

       Moonbeam

          splintered wood.

       Cargo of dread.
       Cargo of hearts

soon to be stopped.

       Memories transported

far from *Heimat*.

       Minds powerless to imagine

                    the methodical mechanics
of   - voidance.

        Squeal   screech

           train stop,

thug flung doors,

        growling sun,
        snarling dogs,
        men barking

              Schnell!

          Schnell!

        Schnell!

The Holocaust

I am afraid.

The Holocaust
no longer scares me.

Distractions, attractions
tempt the mind toward amnesia.

Is there an expiration date
on history's recollection?

Is memory,
the last corpse
of lethal logic?

Proficient hate.
Does the virus survive?
Thrive? Could it revive?

Anno Domini 2019,
many do not recognize
the symptoms of industrialized death:

       trains
       chimneys

       smoke

  medicine inverted.

     Sick odor.
     Sick order.

        Much.

Chambers

Hooks for clothes.
Shoes tied together.
Orderly deceit.

Sauberkeit kommt gleich nach Gottesfurcht.

Showers,
a lethal sleight of hand.

Lonely vast loneliness,
crowded in a chamber emptied of sky,

Now, years later,
poems come from a time-space distance
I never knew. I do not know.
I prefer not knowing.

Thought is cheap and ink is cheap
and making words on paper is easy.

They are other people's words.
I should not write them.
But they must be written.

Words lurch from history's shadows
and I write not to forget,
not to commit the crime of forgetting,
not to commit the sin of understanding
incomprehensible human horror.

We Listened

When the church bell tolled noon, we listened.
When the cuckoo marked the hour, we listened .
When Hans Hotter sang lieder, we listened.
When the Köln city hall carillon played, we listened.
When the choir sang *Ein Feste Burg*, we listened.
When the band marched in the street, we listened.
When the night trains rumbled through, we heard nothing.
When the trains slowed, we heard the cattle speak German.
We heard but did not listen.

'They'

       'They' count.
       'They' can be counted.
       'They' can be discounted.
       'They' don't count.

Divided from humanity.
Added to lists.
Subtracted from life.

Overwhelmed by
stacks of numbers.
stacks of numbers
stacks of numbers
stacks of numbing
numbers

Stacks of numb
       numb
       numb

The King

In the land of the numb
the anesthesiologist is king.

Ballad of 1943

During that fire year
the air sweetened,
soft cinder breezes,
aromatic death.

An overindulgence of murder
but funerals were scarce.

Some children,
considered foes of the future,
were, with their parents,
dispatched into the past.

Pines wore uniforms of ash
to hide their naked green,
the color of hope.

Desperate flowers,
              frantic blooms.

Somehow, still,
many managed to be born.

The Orchestra at Theresienstadt

They lived to play,
and then they played to live,
skillful love of music
now skillful love of life.

Smokescreen,
high culture concealing
the grotesque.

Musicians played Mozart for murderers.

Breath blown through brass and reed,
catgut scratched by stretched strings,
smoldering chords swirl skyward,
dark notes echoed up from ash pages,
a sonata of smoke.

Allegro morphed into
adagio morphed into
death.

The conductor in his black coat,
his back to the gaunt audience,
taunts their ears with symphonic veneers.

Odin at Auschwitz

One people's mythos is
a pretext to slaughter
people of another mythos.

Priests of pandemonium,
vicious liturgies chanted
mystical stench –
incensed smoke,
aromatic atrocity –
magnificat of murder
in basilicas of death-
the ecstasy of brutality--

        rapture.

Native Gods

Up through the plutonic igneous
beds of the ground of the earth
the old cold Nordic gods

                    seep and ooze

in search of animate heat.

They are attracted to warmish
disenchanted blood, *blut-*

      a resurrection

of misplaced

            displaced
            replaced
Götter.

Soul particular to soil,
a people made of clay,

      impressionable

cuneiform - uniform

      bold   mold

a language
of dents and dints
solar and supreme,
superior to a fault.

Lilliputian lords.

Machines

politics makes policy
police impose policy

won't becomes will

patches
labels

arms inked names to numbers
a gargantuan turning
of pretense into past tense

cruel gruel
to fuel human machines

service to servitude
pitiless work

much to less

The Citizen

The little I knew
I didn't want to know.
It would require something
brave of me -
                hurling

my poor words against
the cage of ranting rage.

I knew how not to know,
to misdirect my insightful eye
to see things always seen, and
not see things always never seen.

Once seen, there would be hell to pay.

How to misread signs and signals,
how to be puzzled by the obvious,
how to successfully pretend
black was white,
day was night.
blindness was sight.

Every call forward was an echo back,
except this time with more efficient technology.

I had to learn not to remember
which is not the same as forgetting.
'I will' and 'I will not'
can both be moral choices.

Perhaps in a moral future
I will remember what
I do not want to know.

Master Race

Look at us, and listen.
It is hard to believe we are not superior,
better than the rest, better than the best,

All we wanted was for Jews to self-efface,
give us their place, to make us space,
to respect our privilege as the master race.

All we wanted was for them to disappear.
We were willing to help in any way,
expunge the record of their DNA.

We asked the favor of their absence
so we could bask in the warmth of our
barbed wire bristling twisted sun.

How could we be a master race
without a master plan?

To do this we would
have to call wrong right.

Permission granted.

Utopia

One people's hell,
an island
in another folk's heaven.

Utopia.
Location unknown.

Who lives
there?

And why?

    The worthy?

What criterion?

    Race?
    Religion?
    Ancestors?
    Blood/blut line?

      Save us from
    the wreck
of perfection.

      Save us from
    vile
purity.

Save us for
    democracy's lively

        mess.

What must be destroyed
to make way for *Utopia*?

      Diversity.

Death to diversity!

Long live the mono-minded mass.

Putting Her Children to Bed

Magda Goebbels
put her children to bed
on the night of May 1, 1945.

She herself had been in bed a long time
with their father Joseph Goebbels,
absorbing his contagious dream
from the drool stained pillows
of their mutual sleep.

What he believed, she believed.
What he dreamed, she dreamed.
What he hoped, she hoped.
What he knew, she knew.
What he feared, she feared.

Now in the thundered city,
what they knew and feared was not
what they had hoped and dreamed.

Perhaps, she almost believed
these bodies from her body
would wake up in a better world
where the sin of difference would not be forgiven
and the sin of genocide would be seen as necessity.

Magda kissed each child on the forehead,
their mouths contaminated with death,
an antidote against waking up in
their parent's shattered dream.

A mother's love as she turned out the light,
rescuing her children from a world made of death.

Buchenwald, April, 1945

stacks of silence
unspeakable
death white
bone spilled on bone
flung flesh

    a double muteness:

        silence of the dead
        dead silence of the
        Weimar citizens

What can we say about what wasn't said?
What shall we do with all this silence?
Can we hear without bruising
the anvil in our ear?

We will force complicit silence
to face explicit screams.

The Old SS Guard

I am old.
I am cold.
Flames to ashes
burned memory –
out.

Distraction dwells.
Amnesia swells.

Who am i?
You say that one,
in the photograph,
next to the stacked dead.

My grandson doesn't know
how good we got at death.

A hard brag.

Efficiency,
gas
flame
smoke

so we would not choke
on inconvenient bones.

Poetische Sprache

"There is nothing in the world for which a poet will give up writing, not even when he is a Jew and the language of his poems is German."

Paul Celan (1920-1970)

The mind within my fingers suffers,
I write in the language of my systematic assassins,
Deutsche, guttural, full of phlegm.

I had no better lexikon to state my case against them
than the bundled words they used to murder me,
than the vokabular my neighbors spoke when
teaching math or brewing beer or making love
or inquiring into the nature of being and time.

I tried to learn another tongue to disturb their sleep,
to alert their children to bone ash on windowsills
and blood smeared on doors.

For a time I set aside my pen waiting for a dictionary,
a catalogue of neutral words
that did not bite the hand that wrote them.

The postman arrived each day with no book.

I wrote my poems in the language
babies Adolph H. and Adolph E. learned
while suckling on their mothers' breasts.

Skillfully,
I held their milk black tongues
up to the mirror so they could see
the shadow that they drank.

Concealed among Schiller's lovely nouns and verbs,
a syntax of condemnation slipped from my poet's pen.

I, like Odysseus' sailors clinging to the blinded Cyclops'
sheep,
reversed the tale and entered the monster's cave.

"Did you do these unspeakable things?"
the judge in Jerusalem asked Adolf E.
"No!" the defiant Adolf answered,
"I am Nobody. I just obeyed Somebody's orders."

My name is 'Somebody' now,
I shout into echoing *"Sieg Heils".*

I am the poet of the murdered nameless dead.
I write the silent wails of those whose words
were taken with their breath.
The glossary that lit the flesh-kiln fires now lights my torch,
not to burn,
but to pierce the insufferable smoke-enshrouded Teutonic
dark.

Todtnauberg Hutte July 25, 1967
Paul Celan and Martin Heidegger

Wooden shingles, rafters, roof,
the owner, Martin, German,
and the guest under the beams,
spoke/wrote German like the *Volk*
he almost was but wasn't.

Black wind down the mountain shivers the hut.
Black trees weep.
Black water drips from the pump.
Black light emits from the star on top.
Black earth speaks of grief.

Celan wondered if Heidegger
would speak a word of regret.

      Is there a word,

           enough words

human enough,

      sufficient to relieve titanic silence?

Language first of all, said Martin,
the luring of **is** out of silence,

What Martin knew he could not
and therefore would not say.

             Spoken aloud,
the echo would be endless,

      suffocating,

    asphyxiating.

          Yet,
   no words,

nauseating.

NOTES

Denying the Holocaust

Ludwig von Beethoven (1770-1827) – German composer

Johann Wolfgang von Goethe (1749-1832) – German writer

Johann Christoph Friedrich von Schiller (1759-1805) – German poet

Chameleon

dasein (G) – 'being there', a word used by the philosopher, Martin Heidegger, designating human being, which emphasizes the importance of the place in which a life is situated.

traum (G) – 'dream'

Architect of Hell

Hades – Greek underworld abode of the dead

Charon – ferryman transporting the dead across the River Styx which separates the earth from the underworld

Sheol – Jewish abode of the dead

Valley of Hinnon – a place of execution outside Jerusalem, i.e. Gehenna

Moloch – Canaanite god requiring child sacrifice

The Wannsee Conference: January 20, 1942

die Judenfrage (G) – 'Jewish Question'

Judenfrei (G) – 'free of Jews'

die Endlosung (G) – 'Final Solution'

Night Train to Nowhere

heimat (G) – 'home'

schnell (G) – 'fast'

Chambers

Sauberkeit kommt gleich nach Gottesfurcht (G) – 'cleanliness is next to godliness'

We Listened

Hans Hotter (1909-2003) – a German operatic bass-baritone and Lieder singer and a fervent anti-Nazi.

Ein Feste Burg – *A Mighty Fortress Is Our God*, a hymn by Martin Luther

Native Gods

plutonic – a double meaning; rock formed deep within the earth and realm of Pluto, ruler of the underworld in classic mythology

igneous – heat-formed rock

Putting Her Children to Bed

Magda Goebbels – the wife of the Nazi Minister of Propaganda, Joseph Goebbels, who poisoned her six young

children on the evening of May 1, 1945 before she and her
husband committed suicide.

Poetische Sprache

poetische sprache (G) – 'poetic speech'

The Jewish poet, Paul Celan, lost both parents in the death
camps. He was shaken to the core by the Holocaust, yet
wrote out of his horror and pain in the language that
managed the atrocity: German.

He felt conflicted in this use, but it was his language and as a
poet he could not refuse to write.

First line from Celan's poem *Todesfugue*:
*"Black milk of morning we drink you at dusktime we drink
you at noontime and dawntime we drink you at night"* –

Referring to the Cyclops chapter in *Homer's Odyssey* where
the hero hides his men among the blinded monster's sheep as
they leave the cave. When the Cyclops asked Odysseus his
name, the hero answered 'Nobody' when the Cyclops asks
him to identify himself. When the Cylops neighbors heard
him scream asked who was attacking him, the Cyclops
replied, "Nobody is attacking me."

Todtnauberg Hutte July 25, 1967

Paul Celan and Martin Heidegger

Martin Heidegger (1889-1976) was a 20th century
philosopher. He joined the Nazi Party in 1933 and was
elected rector of Freiberg University. He resigned from the
position in 1934. His affiliation with the Nazi Party cast a
shadow over his work and left mixed opinions about
his contribution to philosophy.

One who saw value in Heidegger's understanding of the
nature of poetry was the Jewish poet Paul Celan
(1920-1970). After giving a reading of his poetry in Freiberg,
the poet and philosopher spent a day together at Heidegger's
cottage near the Black Forest village of Todtnauberg, where

the philosopher wrote many of his books and papers. Celan wrote an enigmatic poem about that day titled *Todtnauberg*.

DESIGN NOTES

In researching period-specific design for the cover, I wondered what approach a print designer in Nazi Germany might have used to publish what would have been — and is today — a rebellious examination of the holocaust. I found an answer in Jan Tschichold's New Typography, a manual describing his radically different approach to print design — one that would ultimately lead to his arrest, followed by him fleeing Germany with his family.

Tschichold believed that modern design should be functional, not decorative. He preferred for the content to speak for itself and chose photography instead of drawings when illustration was needed. Tschichold used contrast, bold lines, shapes, and white space to create asymmetrical layouts with clear hierarchy. He embraced sans serif typefaces instead of the traditional serifs, often using all lower case letters.

Years later, Tschichold abandoned his radical philosophy, acknowledging that it wasn't appropriate for all cases. However, his rebellion and resilience, along with that of many other creatives of the time, made a statement that would outlive his original vision — creativity cannot be extinguished.

Inspired by Tschichold's boldness and bravery, I chose a similar cover design. I want to honor every single person — whether history remembers them or not — who allowed the flame of creativity to live within them during such a dark time. May you feel their courage, warming your heart and strengthening your ability to nurture your own creativity during your darkest moments.

Carter Marshall
Designer